D1798339

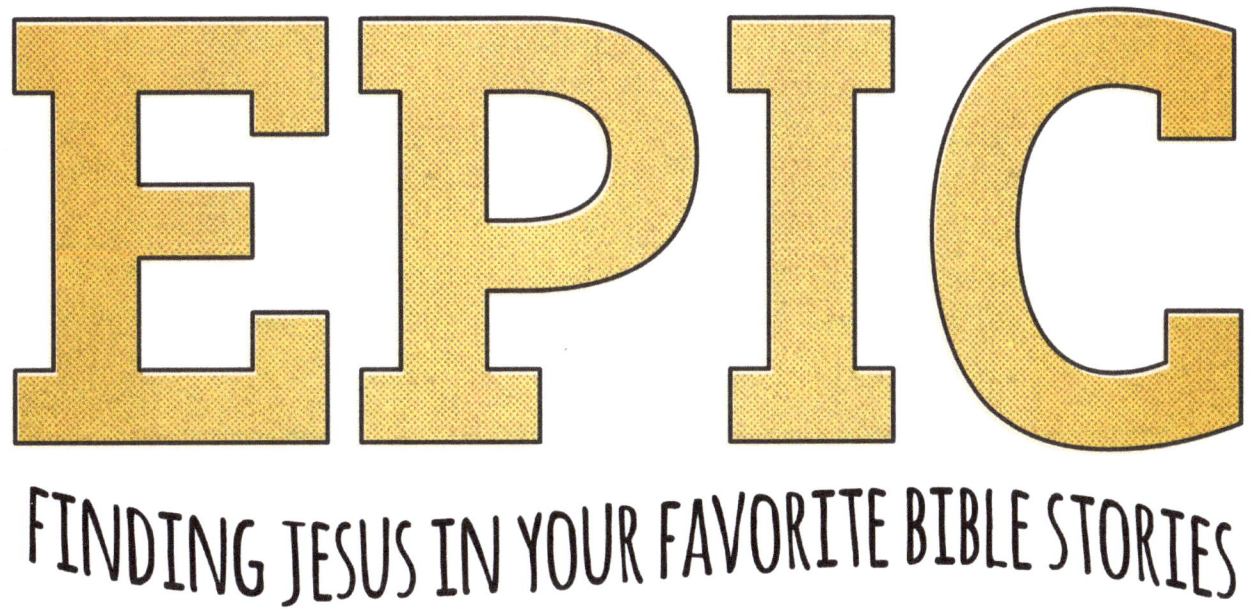

EPIC

FINDING JESUS IN YOUR FAVORITE BIBLE STORIES

CHARLIE GARRISON

ILLUSTRATIONS BY ANDREW LAITINEN

LUCIDBOOKS

Epic

Finding Jesus in Your Favorite Bible Stories

Copyright © 2019 by Charlie Garrison
Illustrations by Andrew Laitinen

Published by Lucid Books in Houston, TX
www.LucidBooksPublishing.com

ISBN-10: 1-63296-393-6
ISBN-13: 978-1-63296-292-8
eISBN-10: 1-63296-291-8
eISBN-13: 978-1-63296-291-1

Special Sales: Most Lucid Books titles are available in special quantity discounts. Custom imprinting or excerpting can also be done to fit special needs. Contact Lucid Books at Info@LucidBooksPublishing.com.

To the most inspiring kids in the world: Leeland, Phoebe, and Gunnar.

"The LORD our God, the LORD is one. Love the LORD your God with all your heart and with all your soul and with all your strength. These commandments that I give you today are to be on your hearts" (Deut. 6:4–6 NIV).

In Jesus's name, Amen.

Table of Contents

Preface

"Noah was a good man."

Anytime I think about Christian children's books, that is the line I remember. I was reading the little cardboard books to my kids before bed, and then it hit me: "Man, these stories are all cool, but I feel like they completely miss the point." So sure, Noah was a good man, but that story wasn't just about him. As I looked through all the children's books I had been reading the kids such as Daniel in the lions' den, David and Goliath, Moses, and Jonah, my feelings were confirmed. It was frightening, but true. You could read these books and never realize that they have anything to do with Jesus.

Every time I would read those books to my kids, I found myself fixing theological issues and pointing each story to Jesus. Shouldn't the book do that? I was blown away.

Each of these stories is amazing in its own right, but there is one Epic story that is weaved throughout all of them: God's plan to send Jesus to earth to secure our salvation. Jesus is and always has been there.

Epic is an attempt to show that all the amazing stories in the Bible that we learn as kids point to Jesus. He is the actual hero of this story. This is His epic story.

Always with Us
Genesis 1–2

Long ago, before anything was created, God lived and was full of love.

God was ready to do something amazing, something . . . epic.

God is good, creative, and powerful. God had so much love to share that he began to create.

And, in the midst of this momentous occasion, Jesus, the Son of God, was there helping with creation! God used words to speak, and things were created.

God said, "Let there be light," and BAM—it was bright!

He said, "Deep oceans go here," and "big mountains go there," and they appeared! He said, "Animals roam here," and they galloped and roared! He said, "Plants grow there," and they grew and bloomed.

God made them beautiful and unique. He made everything just the way He liked it, but He saved His best creation for last. He wanted to share His love with someone who could understand it.

God created a man and a woman. He gave them food to eat, sun for warmth, and comfortable places to sleep. He even gave them a job—to take care of all His creation.

He loved all His creation but especially the man and woman because they were created in the image of God!

Jesus was right there with God all along, and He loved creation too!

"In the beginning was the Word, and the Word was with God, and the Word was God. He was in the beginning with God. All things were made through him, and without him was not anything made that was made" (John 1:1–3).

Jesus is the Word of God. The Son of God helped create everything. He created each person in His image. From the beginning, Jesus shared His love with us.

Always the Plan
Genesis 2–3

God created the first man and the first woman in the Garden of Eden. He named the man Adam. Adam named everything else—the towering giraffes and burly hippos, the blooming flowers and the green trees, even the splashing fish and soaring birds! When Adam saw the woman, he smiled. She was perfect for him. "I will call her Eve," Adam said.

God gave them food and a whole world of plants and animals to take care of. And God gave them each other. God also gave them a warning. "Do not eat from the tree of the knowledge of good and evil. If you eat from that tree, you will die."

"Yikes!" thought Adam. "We will never eat from that tree!"

7

One day, a corkscrew snake with a bad attitude whispered to Eve, "You will not die if you eat fruit from this tree." But this was the tree God had warned them about. The snake was telling lies about God.

"Why would God lie to me?" Eve asked. "But the fruit does look delicious," she thought, "Maybe if I take just one bite, God won't mind." She chose to believe the serpent instead of God. She took a bite. Then she gave the fruit to Adam, and he ate it too.

In that moment, evil rushed into the world. God was heartbroken. His beloved creation didn't trust Him. They did not listen to God's warning. They disobeyed. That is what sin is.

"Adam, Eve," God said. "You must leave the garden. I love you, but I cannot be around your sin." Everybody was very sad.

Yet, God is a God of good news, not bad news. God had a plan.

He said to the serpent, "Someday, I will send my son Jesus to defeat you. You will strike His heel, but He will crush your head."

Eventually, good would overcome evil. Sin would be defeated. Even though Jesus died on the cross, He was resurrected three days later. He defeated the devil. That's good news.

"He himself bore our sins" in his body on the cross, so that we might die to sins and live for righteousness; "by his wounds you have been healed" (1 Peter 2:24 NIV).

God always had a plan to defeat evil. The way for good to defeat evil doesn't lie in us, but in Jesus dying on the cross. When Jesus died, God was showing His love for everybody. Now, when anybody puts their faith in Jesus, they receive God's promise to be with Him again.

That's good news.

Always Makes a Way
Genesis 6–9

God loves His creation, but His creation doesn't always love Him back.

Sin entered the world, and people stopped obeying God. They hurt each other. But God had a plan to save people. Even when we do something bad and are in trouble, God makes a way for us to be saved. He is always saving, even if we don't deserve it.

God came to Noah and said, "Noah! I am going to send a flood over the whole earth. I have chosen you and your family to survive."

Noah replied, "Uhh . . . why us God? What have I done to deserve this?"

"Nothing," God replied. "I have given you favor and grace. Make the biggest boat the world has ever seen. I will save you, your family, and two of every kind of animal on the earth. When the rain comes, you will be safe in the ark."

Noah was blown away, but he believed God and did what He said to do. He built the biggest boat the world had ever seen.

12

Drip, drop, splash. The rain started coming down. It poured.

Strike—went the lightning! Boom—went the thunder! The ocean splashed. The wind whirled, and the rain wouldn't quit! Noah and the animals were nervous because the ocean water kept rising.

Water blanketed the earth, but safe in the ark, Noah and his family and all the animals were thankful. God had saved them!

After 40 days, the rain stopped. As the water slowly crept back into place, deep blue oceans formed, and there was dry land again!

When Noah stepped out of the boat and onto land, he worshiped God for saving him and his family.

"Noah, I promise never to do that again," said God. Then God painted the sky! Red, orange, blue, green, purple, and pink stretched from the edge of the sky to the top of the mountains—the first rainbow!

Rainbows remind us of God's promise to make a way for us to be saved.

Jesus said, "I am the door. If anyone enters by me, he will be saved and will go in and out and find pasture" (John 10:9).

Jesus is like an ark saving us from a flood. No matter what, when we believe in Jesus, we get to be with God forever! God always makes a way for us to be saved.

Always Keeps His Promises
Genesis 17–18

After God painted the sky for Noah,
God made another promise, this time
to a man named Abram. God and
Abram made a covenant—a forever
promise that God would never break.

God said to Abram, "Move your family
to a new land. I will make you a father
with kids all over the world. Your family
will outnumber the stars in the sky!"

But Abram and his wife Sarai were
pretty old, and they didn't have
any kids, yet.

"How will we have as many kids as
the stars if we don't even have one?"
they asked. Still, they believed
God's promise.

God said, "I will establish my covenant
between me and you and your offspring
after you throughout their
generations for an everlasting
covenant, to be God to you and
to your offspring after you." God was
making them part of His family.

Then God changed Abram's name to
Abraham, which means "father of
many." Sarai's name became Sarah,
meaning "mother of nations."

18

Sarah gave birth to a baby. Abraham and Sarah named the baby Isaac. Then Isaac had kids, and his kids had kids, and before you knew it, God had made a giant group of people called the Israelites! God was their God, and they were God's people.

Thousands of years later, Jesus was born. He was part of Abraham's family, too. Jesus came to make their enormously giant family even bigger. Everyone who believes in Him is a part of God's family. Today, God's family outnumbers the stars in the sky! God never breaks a promise.

"Christ redeemed us from the curse of the law by becoming a curse for us—for it is written, 'Cursed is everyone who is hanged on a tree'—so that in Christ Jesus the blessing of Abraham might come to the Gentiles, so that we might receive the promised Spirit through faith" (Galatians 3:13–14).

God loves people and promises to save everyone who believes in Jesus as their Savior. And God never breaks a promise!

Always Freeing
Exodus 7–14

Hundreds of years later, the Israelites were enslaved in Egypt. God wanted His people to be free.

Moses was in the desert when, with a crackle and a booming voice, God spoke to him as a burning bush. "Moses, I want you to tell Pharaoh, the King of Egypt, to set my people free. Then you will lead them into the land that I promised to give to Abraham and his family."

Moses knew the voice in the burning bush was God, but Moses wasn't a warrior or a leader. He was just a shepherd. He said, "God, I can't do that. I'm not a leader."

But if God can make a burning bush talk, He can make a leader out of a shepherd.

God sent Moses to Pharaoh, the king of Egypt, to tell him to set the Israelites free.

Moses said, "Let my people go!"

Pharaoh laughed and said, "No way!"

God sent giant bugs to Egypt to eat their food. He turned their blue rivers into red blood. He sent frogs hopping into houses. He made it rain ice. He sent hot fevers and itchy rashes on all the Egyptians.

Every time God sent a plague, Moses pleaded with Pharaoh, "Just let my people go, and these terrible things will stop."

Pharaoh refused.

Moses warned Pharaoh over and over again, but he wouldn't budge. One night, God sent His final punishment and wiped out all the firstborn boys in Egypt except for the Israelites. God was not happy that He had to send the final punishment, but finally, Pharaoh let God's people go.

As Moses and the Israelites fled Egypt, Pharaoh sent his army after them. They chased the Israelites to the Red Sea. The Israelites were trapped!

God said, "Moses, put your staff in the water, and I will rescue you." As Moses put his staff into the water, the sea roared and opened up, creating two giant walls of water and a path for all God's people to walk through! As the Israelites hurried to the other side, Moses looked into the walls of water and saw beautiful fish, mean sharks, graceful turtles, and bright coral.

"What a rescue," Moses thought.

The Egyptian army hurried to follow them through the sea, but when Moses arrived on the other side, God released the walls of water. The water crashed down, swallowing up that great big army!

"For freedom Christ has set us free; stand firm therefore, and do not submit again to a yoke of slavery" (Galatians 5:1).

God is always freeing people. He led the Israelites out of Egypt with a path to freedom through the Red Sea. And God sent His son, Jesus, to earth to set us free from our sins. Jesus will stop at nothing to save us! He gave up His life to make sure we are set free. Our path to freedom is believing in Jesus.

Always Victorious
1 Samuel 17

God's people finally had their own land called Israel, and it was great! People were really happy!

One Israelite boy who lived in Bethlehem was a shepherd named David. David trusted God with all his heart. He loved God, and God was always with him.

One day, an army from Philistia attacked the Israelite army. A huge and powerful Philistine warrior named Goliath yelled out, "Send your best warrior to fight me!"

"No way!" The Israelites were terrified. Even the powerful Israelite king, Saul, shook with fear. They needed a warrior who could defeat Goliath. They needed a victor.

When David heard about Goliath, he said, "I'll fight him! He is not fighting against me, but against God!"

David took his slingshot and five stones. He marched to the battlefield.

Goliath laughed at the young shepherd. "You're sending a little boy to fight me with rocks. This will be easy!"

HA HA HA

HA HA HA

29

David wasn't laughing. He believed God had won the fight already. "Surely if God went to the trouble of making a people for Himself, God will protect them from this giant!" thought David. "The battle is the Lord's."

David placed a stone in his slingshot, whirled it over his head. The stone sailed through the air. Kapow! The stone struck Goliath in the head, and just like that, the battle was over!

David defeated Goliath! God's people were saved. God had sent them a victor.

"Trust in the Lord with all your heart and lean not on your own understanding; in all your ways submit to him, and he will make your paths straight" (Proverbs 3:5–6).

There is a victor for us all—Jesus! Our sin is so giant that without God's help, there's no way we can defeat it. Jesus has to win that battle for us, just like David won the battle for his people. Jesus saves everyone who believes in Him. The battle is the Lord's.

Always Faithful
Daniel 6

Around 600 BC, the Babylonians enslaved the Israelites. Slavery again! Faithful Daniel, who prayed to God three times every day, became a slave in the court of the king. He felt afraid, but he knew God would save His people.

The king was having troubling dreams.

"I know what your dreams mean," said Daniel. This made the king feel better. He liked the good advice Daniel gave him, too.

Daniel became the lead adviser to the king.

Years passed, and a new king came into power, King Darius. Darius loved Daniel because he was faithful, and God was with him.

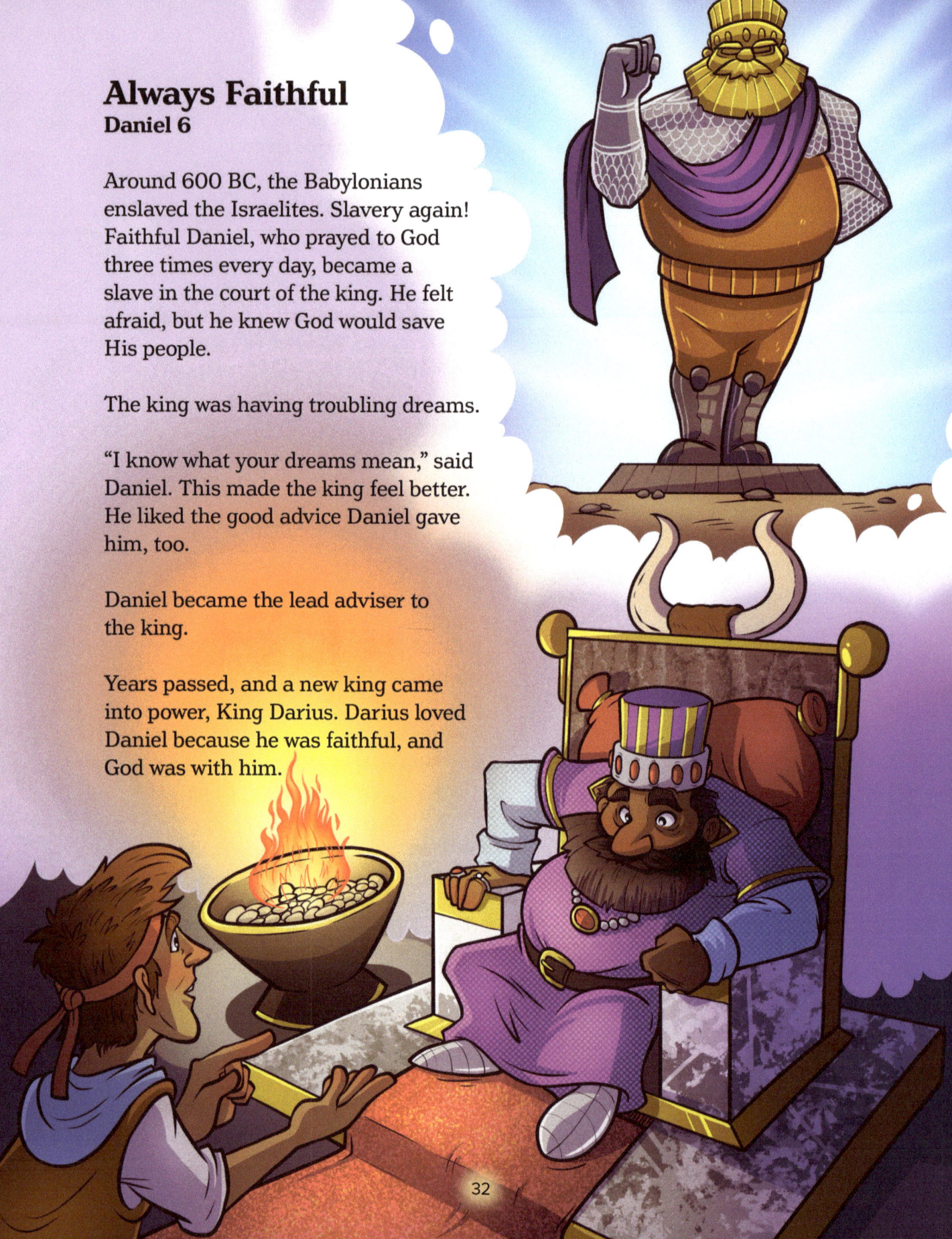

"The king likes Daniel more than us," whined another adviser.

"Yeah! First, Daniel took our job, and now he's our boss!" cried another. "What are we going to do?"

"Let's make a law that will get him in trouble," they said. They began plotting.

"Since Daniel prays to his God three times every day, let's make a law that everybody must pray to King Darius only! Anyone who doesn't obey the law will be fed to the lions."

"This law is outstanding!" said King Darius.

Even though it meant breaking the new law, faithful Daniel kept praying to God three times every day.

"Now we've got him!" thought the royal advisers. "Daniel has broken the law! He prayed to the God of the Israelites, not to you," they said to King Darius. "We must throw him into the lions' den!"

Even though King Darius liked Daniel, he agreed that the law must be obeyed. Into the lions' den went Daniel!

The lions prowled. There was nowhere to hide, nowhere to run. What could Daniel do? He was scared.

The lions roared.
"God, help me!" Daniel prayed.

Suddenly, a powerful angel of God appeared and shut the mouths of the lions. Their roars and snarls changed to purrs and meows. Safe, Daniel slept peacefully through the night.

In his kingly bed, Darius couldn't sleep. He felt terrible.

The next morning, the king awoke in a panic. "How could I have let Daniel be fed to the lions?" He dashed to the lions' den.

Daniel yelled, "God saved me! I'm alive!"

What a relief! King Darius was enraged when he found out that the advisers had made the law just to get rid of Daniel.

"Guards! Throw the other leaders to the lions!" Darius shouted. "They tricked me. I'm making a new law," said Darius. "Everybody must worship Daniel's God. He is a God who saves!"

"He will swallow up death forever; and the Lord GOD will wipe away tears from all faces, and the reproach of his people he will take away from all the earth, for the LORD has spoken" (Isaiah 25:8).

The lions seemed like a sure death for Daniel, but God saved him. Just like Daniel, Jesus lived His life faithful to God the Father. When Jesus died and rose again on the third day, He had triumphed over death! Now, when you believe in Jesus, God promises to give you life forever in heaven. He will save you!

Always Working
Jonah 1–4

God loves sending people to teach others about Him. One day, God gave Jonah a job.

"Jonah," God said, "go to Nineveh and tell the Ninevites about me."

"Not the Ninevites!" Jonah thought. "The Ninevites are ferocious!"

So, Jonah ran away. He hid from God on a boat sailing far away from Nineveh.

"Fine," thought God. "If you think the sea can hide you from Me, I will send a mighty storm to show that you cannot run from what I have called you to."

The big blue waves turned dark. Water crashed, and wind whooshed! Side to side the boat rocked. Over the waves, it jumped and slammed back down into the water. The boat was going to sink! Everybody on the boat was in danger.

"This is my fault," Jonah thought. He told the sailors to toss him into the sea. "God will calm the storm and save you," he told them. So, the sailors pitched Jonah into the dangerous waters.

Just as he said, the storm slept. Jonah never expected what God would do next.

God sent a colossal fish to swallow Jonah, but not to eat him—to save him! Gulp! The fish swallowed Jonah.

"Yuck!" shouted Jonah in the dark and stinky belly of the big fish. Dead sea creatures, bits of boats, and rotten seaweed floated around inside.

As he sloshed around, Jonah realized the fish was sent by God to save him. He prayed, "God, I will go wherever You send me."

After three days, God made the big fish spit Jonah out on the beach. Bleerrpp!!! Now, Jonah was ready to work with God! On to Nineveh he marched.

Jonah told the Ninevites about God, and they all believed!

"For we are God's handiwork, created in Christ Jesus to do good works, which God prepared in advance for us to do" (Ephesians 2:10 NIV).

God used the big fish to put Jonah on a path back to His calling. God had a plan to bring more people into His family, and He used Jonah to make that happen. God does the same thing today! Just like God sent the big fish, God sent Jesus to rescue us. People may try to hide like Jonah did, but God sees us, saves us, and works through us. When we believe in Jesus, we are saved to do good work!

Always about the Good News
By Connie Hartman
Luke 2

Many, many years passed. Hundreds, actually. God's people served Him patiently while He prepared the next part of His epic love story.

Mary, a Jewish girl, lived in the quiet town of Nazareth. She was engaged to Joseph. Mary and Joseph were looking forward to beginning their life together in Nazareth.

God delighted in Mary. She was faithful and humble.

One night, God sent His top messenger, the angel Gabriel, to visit Mary. God had an important job for her.

"Mary," said the angel Gabriel. "Don't be scared. You are favored by God. He has chosen you to be the mother of Jesus, His Son, who will rescue God's people. Jesus will be their King forever."

Mary was very surprised!

"I belong to the Lord. I will follow Him and do all that He asks of me," she told Gabriel.

It all came down to this. All the stories in the Bible had been pointing to Jesus and His love for us. He was finally arriving!

When it came time for Mary to give birth to Jesus, they were on a long trip to Bethlehem. Bethlehem had been the hometown of King David a long, long time ago. Many people were there. Mary and Joseph looked and looked, but they couldn't find a place to stay in the whirling city.

Joseph frantically asked different people, "Excuse me. Do you have room for us to stay in tonight? My wife is going to have a baby."

Time after time, people said, "No."

"God," they prayed, "We really need You. Please help us with a place to stay."

Finally, one innkeeper said, "I don't have room, but you can sleep in the stable." Mary and Joseph had to rest on the itchy hay with the cows, sheep, and donkeys, but God was with them. They eagerly prepared for the birth of Jesus. They couldn't wait for Him to arrive!

That night, in a stable in Bethlehem, the most magical thing happened. The Savior of the world was born!

When Jesus's first tiny baby cries reached to the heavens, God and His angels rejoiced! They exploded with excitement and joy. The Savior had entered the world!

"Glory to God in the highest!" shouted the angels. "Peace on earth to those who God favors!"

"And the angel said to them, 'Fear not, for behold, I bring you good news of great joy that will be for all the people. For unto you is born this day in the city of David a Savior, who is Christ the Lord'" (Luke 2:10–11).

Mary treasured this good news. Jesus is the best gift any of us can receive! This baby would grow up to heal the sick, make the blind see, and forgive us for our sins. On Christmas Day and every day, take a minute to treasure the gift of Jesus's forgiveness and love.

Always Loving
The Gospels

When Jesus grew up, he made many friends. Some of his friends, who called themselves his disciples, walked everywhere with Jesus. Wherever they walked, He showed them how to love God and all the people they met. He prayed, took care of people, and obeyed God.

He explained how to follow God, "You should love God, love people, and treat them the way that you want to be treated."

When people asked, "How do we get to be with God forever?" He answered, "The only way to God is to believe in Me."

When He saw sick people, He would touch them, and bam! They were all better. He made blind people see by rubbing mud on their eyes! When He saw people who couldn't walk, He shouted, "Get up and walk!" And they jumped for joy!

Jesus was special, and everybody knew it!

"Wow!" thought His disciples. "Jesus is awesome! How could we ever live like Jesus?"

Jesus said, "You're going to do all the things I'm doing and even greater things!"

Some religious leaders didn't like what Jesus was doing and teaching. They didn't know that He was the one about whom all the epic stories in scripture were written.

Jesus told them, "You worry too much about things that are not even important and pay no attention to loving and helping people."

The religious leaders made a plan to arrest Jesus, but He kept on teaching and healing.

"Therefore, if anyone is in Christ, he is a new creation. The old has passed away; behold, the new has come" (2 Corinthians 5:17).

This is how Jesus wanted everybody to live. He knew it would be hard to love everyone and treat people the way that you want to be treated. When we believe in Jesus, He makes it possible to love God and love other people just like He did.

Always Saving
Matthew 26–28

Jesus lived a life of healing, teaching, making friends, and helping people! But, since before the beginning of time, God had something even greater planned.

Jesus said, "I came to give My life so that many people could be saved."

One night, after one last meal with His friends, a group of Roman soldiers arrested Jesus. Powerful people didn't like the way He was teaching, healing people, and saying that He is the only way to God.

Things were getting very tense, but this is the moment God had been planning forever. God was going to fix the problem created by every person since Adam and Eve ate the fruit in the garden. God would solve the problem of sin. He would show once and for all how much He loves people.

After He was arrested, some of the Jewish leaders who didn't like Jesus demanded that Roman soldiers crucify Him. Crucifixion was a really painful way to die.

The soldiers made fun of Jesus. "Some King you are!" They whipped Him and beat Him. It was the most horrible pain He had ever experienced. But Jesus didn't argue. He didn't fight back. He knew this was the only way for people to be forgiven for their sins.

On the very worst Friday, Jesus died on a cross for everyone's sins. The disciples felt heartbroken and terrified for their own lives.

After Jesus died, His friends placed His body in a tomb.

But just when all seemed lost, something amazing happened. Three days later, women who had been friends of Jesus visited His tomb. When they arrived, His body was gone! Alarmed, they asked, "Where is He?"

An angel appeared, saying "He is not here! He is risen!" Astonished, Jesus's friends scampered back to shout it out that He was alive. Jesus overcame death!

The hearts of his followers swelled with hope. Jesus died so that people can live forever with God. He proved it by coming back to life!

Earlier, Jesus had said to His followers, "I am the resurrection and the life. Whoever believes in me, though he die, yet shall he live, and everyone who lives and believes in me shall never die. Do you believe this?" (John 11:25–26).

Jesus loves us so much that He died for us. His amazing sacrifice, in dying for all of us, wasn't the end! Jesus defeated death and is alive again!

Always Shining
Acts

The story wasn't finished.

After Jesus rose from the dead, He stayed with His friends for forty days. He gave His followers a job and made them a promise.

"Remember when I said you will do even greater things than Me?" Jesus asked. "I am going back to heaven. I will send you the Holy Spirit. When you receive the Spirit, go! Tell people everywhere about Me! It's your turn to make disciples."

Then Jesus returned to heaven to be with God forever.

Just like Jesus promised, the Holy Spirit came to the disciples. They spoke in every language saying, "Believe in Jesus! Follow Him! Love one another!"

Jesus wanted disciples who made disciples who made more disciples! He wanted them to shine the light of His good news like a light in the dark, brightening the entire world with love and forgiveness.

We believe in Jesus today because somebody told us about Him!

Each one of us who believes in Jesus has a job, the same job Jesus gave to His disciples. He wants you—yes, you—to shine the light of His love. He promises to be with you; to send you the Holy Spirit; and give you courage, peace, and faith no matter what!

The Holy Spirit gives you courage and strength to do the job God has given you!

"Go therefore and make disciples of all nations, baptizing them in the name of the Father and of the Son and of the Holy Spirit, teaching them to observe all that I have commanded you. And behold, I am with you always, to the end of the age" (Matthew 28:19–20).

You have your own chapter in this epic story. Are you ready to keep the story going? Go and shine!

It's going to be epic!

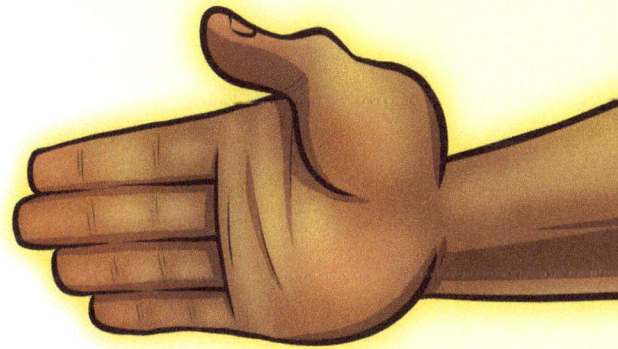

Acknowledgments

First, I thank Jesus: This book is about You. Use it to Your Glory.

Birge, you're everything. Words cannot express my love for you. You're my partner in everything. You encourage these crazy adventures that I take us on. Thank you for always loving me and helping keep our family pointed in the right direction. There's more to come!

Garrison 3, you are the reason for this book. Love Jesus and do epic things for the kingdom.

Con-dog, I appreciate you so much. Your contribution to this project is huge; I truly couldn't have done it without you. Thanks for being a better writer than me, always helping with edits and contributing the Christmas story.

Mike Larsen, I wouldn't have written this if you hadn't convinced me. You're the man.

The Well Church, thanks for continually having babies that you can read this to. Your kiddos are a huge part of the reason I wrote this thing. May it bless your families.

Larry and Lisa, you guys believe in me. I don't know if you understand how huge that is. Your reach goes far beyond what you see. I know I'm not the only one who feels this way.

Matt Schartz, for helping me fall in love with kids' ministry before I even believed in Jesus.

My parents, you guys are the most supportive parents I could ever imagine. Thanks for being an example.

Jonathan and Kristen, your generosity and belief in me nourishes my soul. Keep making a kingdom impact in all you do.

Sara, my editor. You stretched me and made this book readable. Thank you for being an advocate for the reader.

Cory, my brother. I'm so proud of the man you are. Thanks for your undying support.

CPSIA information can be obtained
at www.ICGtesting.com
Printed in the USA
BVHW021037120419
545356BV00017B/188/P